Retain Talent

Through

Learning and Development

Bryan Law

Fox College of Business

First edition: January 2023

Fox College of Business

Disclaimer

Fox College of Business and Bryan Law are not engaged in rendering legal, accounting, investment, or other professional services. This book should not be relied upon as providing such advice. We strongly urge that you seek professional advice before acting on the information contained herein.

The information contained herein has been obtained from sources that we believe are reliable, but we cannot guarantee its accuracy or completeness. Fox College of Business, Bryan Law, and every person involved in creating this book disclaim any warranty as to the accuracy, completeness, and currency of the contents of this book. We also disclaim all liability with respect to the results of any action taken or not taken based upon information in this book.

Bryan Law B.Math., LL.M., LL.D.

Bryan is an entrepreneur with a diversified professional background. He has over 25 years of experience in strategy, analysis, franchise, education, learning and development. Besides being a management consultant, Bryan is a legal researcher in various areas, including contract, environmental, human rights, labour, privacy, and real estate law.

He was a certified instructor, professor, and legal and real estate subject matter expert at various business colleges and education providers. He provided one-on-one training to the management levels in corporations, including C-level executives in public companies.

He authored over 40 books on various topics, including management, real estate, creative thinking, entrepreneurship and human rights. Bryan's wide-ranging knowledge, professional experience, and excellent training and coaching skills have made him one of Canada's foremost management consultants and trainers.

Table of Contents

1. Introduction

Human resources are the most important capital of a corporation. Even for a 100% automated factory controlled by artificial intelligence, maintenance work for the building, machinery, software, and supplies is performed by humans. The word "talent" is used in the field to label good employees. However, their experiences, skills, and values are the actual qualifiers for assessing them. Finding effective and efficient ways to acquire, retain and manage great talents becomes one of the most challenging jobs of an organization, and that rests on the shoulders of the human resources professionals.

The functions of a human resources department may include hiring and recruitment, learning and development, employer-employee relations, employee benefits, compliance, career planning, rewards and recognition, and dealing with complaints and performance issues. They fall into four major duties – talent acquisition, talent development, talent management and talent retention. Some functions may fall under more than one duty. For example, career planning is under talent development, talent management and talent retention. On the other hand, learning and development are under talent development and talent retention.

Talent acquisition involves hiring and recruitment, employer-employee relations, employee benefits, compliance and career planning. When there is a vacancy, HR needs to hire a candidate. However, planned hiring is required to meet expansion plans, which is the recruitment process. Employer-employee relations are under talent acquisition when a labour union is involved, or a special arrangement is needed for the recruit. Competitive employee benefits attract talent and make the recruitment process more manageable.

Talent development involves learning and development, career planning, rewards and recognition, and dealing with complaints and performance issues. The market is constantly changing, so an organization and its employees must develop together. When employees are trained and contribute to the organization, they need rewards, recognition and advancement in their career paths. The human resources department should give employees a hand when facing issues obstructing their performance or development.

Talent management involves employer-employee relations, employee benefits, compliance, career planning, and dealing with complaints and performance issues. In addition to each department manager, the human resources department needs to know the strengths and weaknesses of each employee so they can re-assign their positions if needed. That is crucial for a project-based working environment. HR needs to maintain and cultivate relationships with labour unions and their members, especially for the changes and terminations of employment. HR must also manage compliance, career planning, complaints and performance issues.

Talent retention involves learning and development, employer-employee relations, employee benefits, compliance, career planning, rewards and recognition, and dealing with complaints and performance issues. HR must do well in career planning, rewards and recognition to retain talent. Compliance with labour law and essential employee benefits are the fundamentals of retaining employees. Learning and development play crucial roles in talent retention, too.

Being a management consultant, I am often involved in different stages of talent acquisition, development, retention and management. Most clients would hire permanent full-time positions, while some would hire part-time or independent contractors. Exploring the means to retain talent is HR professionals' most challenging task, especially for part-time staff and independent contractors. Over time, I found that learning and development is an excellent way for employees to develop their careers and for the organization to retain talent.

2. Reasons for Talent Loss

There are many reasons for employees to quit their jobs. Other than personal issues, the reasons for an organization losing employees are classified into two main categories – external (outside the organization) and internal (within the organization).

External Factors for Talent Loss

External factors are out of the control of an HR department and the organization itself. They include national political turmoil, economic downturn, foreign countries providing a better quality of life, foreign regions providing more favourable career opportunities, and other organizations offering more favourable career opportunities.

Political Turmoil

When a country is in a state of political instability, its citizens may not want to stay. Many may flee the country and cause a brain drain in all organizations – government agencies, for-profit and nonprofit organizations. The situation will be worse if the workforce is heavily dependent on foreigners.

Economic Downturn

An economic downturn can lead to a wave of unemployment. Many organizations, including governments, may have to lay off some employees due to the poor economy. Unless the organization outperforms the overall economy and can maintain its workforce, it will lose some of its talents due to the economic downturn. Those laid-off talents may have to leave the country to find jobs, and the local job market will lack a workforce once the economy improves.

A Better Quality of Life in Foreign Countries

In today's world economy, population mobility is exceptionally high. All countries must compete for talent because people constantly seek a better quality of life. Sometimes, people go to work in another country just because of a lower income tax rate, sometimes because of a lower crime rate or a more affordable standard of living. That also applies to different regions. Brain drain is common in developing countries because people may find a better quality of life abroad.

Favourable Career Opportunities in Foreign Regions

Due to staffing shortages, some cities or regions may be willing to offer more attractive packages for workers from overseas. For example, China provided extremely high salaries to recruit pilots decades ago. In 2021, the United Kingdom offered 5,000 work visas to foreigners to tackle a shortage of truck drivers. When a region provides more favourable career opportunities to outsiders, it will draw away some talents from other areas.

Favourable Career Opportunities from Other Organizations

There has always been competition for talent among different organizations. Organizations that attract talent are not necessarily rivals in the field; they may be in other industries. For example, every organization needs accounting, human resources, and IT professionals, and the government sector becomes a target for commercial organizations competing for talent.

Internal Factors for Talent Loss

The external factors above affect an organization, especially its human resources department. However, those factors cannot be changed by the organization. On the other hand, internal factors that cause talent loss may be fixed by the organization, especially the human resources department. Those factors may include a poor outlook for the organization, dissatisfaction with organizational culture, unpleasant or unsafe job types, toxic work environments, and unattractive compensation packages. Internal factors may also include the lack of promotion opportunities or recognition, lack of job satisfaction, feeling overworked or lack of support, need for better work-life balance, and unhappiness with their managers.

Outlook is Not Optimistic

When the outlook for an organization is not optimistic, the first thing associated with it is layoffs. Even if the organization has no plan to cut its workforce, the employees may not want to wait for the layoffs and will proactively look for another job. As a result, the organization suffers from talent loss.

The performance of an organization is in the hands of the management team, not the human resources department. However, the human resources department can move people around to help the organization operate and grow more efficiently.

Dissatisfaction with Organizational Culture

A healthy and constructive culture is crucial for an organization. Not all employees can work in an environment under high pressure that looks only for good results. Like the work environment, organizational culture may be toxic, especially when the management is aggressive or result-oriented. If the organizational culture is terrible, it will cause employees to leave.

The culture of an organization is established or developed by management. If the culture is toxic, management has no excuse and must correct it. The human resources department can help the organization be more inclusive and harmonious by implementing appropriate EDI (Equity, Diversity and Inclusive) policies.

Unpleasant or Unsafe Work Type

Some jobs are disgusting, such as mortician and toilet attendant. The former has to deal with mental challenges, and the latter has to endure unpleasant odours and a dirty work environment. Some jobs are dangerous, such as fishing and construction workers. Both have to work on heavy machinery and face high fatality rates. Many people will quit, especially the new recruits.

Although the nature of work or work environment may not change, there may be things organizations can do to improve working conditions. For example, an organization might provide employees with masks, gloves, protective clothing, or psychotherapy. Of course, compliance with the relevant occupational health and safety laws is a minimum requirement that the human resources department must ensure.

Low Compensation Package

Money is not everything, but almost everything needs it. A base salary, medical benefits, annual leave and sick leave with pay are the minimum compensation package for full-time employees in most countries. Good talents deserve much more than the minimum compensation package; otherwise, they will quit.

Many big organizations will do benchmark studies to assess whether their compensation packages for different employee levels are attractive. The question is how high is enough to retain good talents. Sometimes, the total compensation package is not measurable, at least not by money. For example, some organizations offer flexible work hours or work-from-home options that are attractive to employees and are not measurable by money. Learning and development are other ways to retain talent, with an emphasis on development.

Toxic Work Environment

When a work environment is full of negative behaviours, such as manipulation, bullying, yelling, and discrimination, it is called a toxic one. No one will enjoy working in such an environment. Unlike terrible organizational culture, which starts from the top management and applies to the whole organization, a toxic work environment can arise and exist at any level or workplace alone.

Most people believe a toxic work environment is created by coworkers as they participate in those negative behaviours. The causes of unhealthy work environments may differ, but they share one thing in common – the management tolerates them. Good managers will never allow their work environment to become toxic. The human resources department should ensure all managers would not allow a toxic culture to develop within their department by setting rules and providing appropriate learning and development programs to educate them.

Lack of Promotion Opportunities

Most employees would look for a promotion, even though many do not have a well-planned career path. Suppose the structure of an organization is too simple and has only a few levels for its employees to develop their careers. In that case, they will look for external opportunities for better development.

A human resources department should have plans to create better job descriptions, job titles and company structure to ensure the organization has enough room for employees to develop their careers. A well-planned learning and development program is crucial for employees to gain knowledge and give back to the organization. It is an excellent tool for developing the employees' careers as well.

Lack of Job Satisfaction

Not all kinds of jobs can provide satisfaction to employees. Many entry-level positions, such as receptionist, janitor, and driver, are routine and lack promotion opportunities. Suppose a person does not expect to work routinely but eventually has to do a tedious job. In that case, it is not easy to retain that person, at least not for that position.

It is hard to turn a boring job into an interesting one. A position with a slim chance of promotion is not attractive to most people. Both kinds of jobs would cause the employees to leave. However, a plaque or certificate can serve as a token of appreciation with or without monetary reward. It can be a good morale booster when there is no room for promoting the staff. They can be granted every year to recognize the service provided by the employees without setting a target to be achieved.

Feeling Overworked

Every employee, even the top management, may have experienced or felt overworked. Too much stress is the most common reason people quit their jobs, as health is their top priority, and people cannot work well without healthy physical and mental conditions. Sometimes, the workload can be spread among coworkers or delegated to subordinates, but the process or procedure may be complex and need support from HR and management.

The human resources department and all department heads should periodically review the workloads of their employees and ensure all employees, including top management, will not be overloaded. A better work-life balance is essential to every employee in the organization and should be promoted as the top priority.

Feeling Unsupported

Everyone needs support from others to do their jobs well. The support may be from customers, coworkers, managers and subordinates. When an employee feels there is a lack of support, it causes stress, frustration, and lack of confidence and hinders the performance of that employee. Eventually, the employee would leave the organization due to feeling unsupported.

Team spirit and an inclusive organizational culture are essential to creating a supportive environment that promotes relationships of trust and respect among customers, employees and management. Suitable training programs can help the teams build their spirit and know the importance of supporting each other.

Unhappiness with Management

Although many employees may have known the organizational culture, employee benefits, work policies, rules and regulations well before joining the organization, some may not be familiar with them and may be disappointed after learning them. Since those policies are all set up by management and can be changed over time, some employees may not be happy with the changes made by the management. As a result, they may change their jobs to work for other organizations which have better policies or do not have similar policies.

Management also includes managers at all levels. Employees may resign because of their immediate supervisor rather than top management. Some managers have preferences for their team members, which can lead to unfair treatment of other team members who are not part of the manager's preferences. That is one of the leading causes of employees quitting. Many employees leave their jobs because of their department managers, not because of top management.

A great manager is one who can manage people well. Not all managers know how to manage people. They may be top performers in their departments, such as top salespersons, but they lack management skills. The human resources department should ensure that all managers have completed appropriate training programs before managing people. That is one of the reasons why learning and development play a crucial role in talent retention.

Other Reasons

All the above are the common reasons that employees leave their organization. There are other reasons behind that, including personal reasons. Unfortunately, many employees would not tell their managers the problems that they are facing, especially personal problems.

Communication between employees and management is essential. The organization would not be able to fix the problems without knowing them. Sometimes, the organization can solve the employees' personal issues by giving them flexibility. For example, some employees want to quit their jobs because of time conflicts. They need to take care of their children or elderly at home and thus cannot work full-time or regular hours. If the managers know about that and the organization can offer flexible working hours or part-time positions, those employees may not have to quit.

Even after an employee has quit, it is crucial to know the reasons behind it. An exit interview can provide the organization with invaluable insight into the employee perspective of the organization and particular reasons for their leaves. It can also help determine whether its employee retention strategies need any improvement.

3. The Role of Learning and Development

Some terms have been changed in the human resources field, with reasons. The change of name is due to the evolution of the responsibilities of the department. The term "Human Resources" was called "Personnel" in the past. Personnel refers to the actual human beings (Humans), but an organization needs to recruit, train, develop and manage people to be better Resources. The human resources department is responsible for building an organization with great people and programs. Another way to tell the difference between the two names is that the functions of a personnel department are reactive, while the functions of a human resources department are proactive.

A similar logic applies to the name Learning and Development. It started with the term Training first. An organization needs to train its staff to perform their jobs, especially those that require special skills, such as the police force. They have a unique operation protocol that other organizations may not have. Once the human resources professionals found that Development is a crucial factor for employees' careers, which is also one of the purposes of training their staff, the term Training and Development was used.

Employees who receive training are in passive mode. They just learn what the trainers teach. Therefore, the term is changed to Learning and Development, emphasizing how much the employees learn but not how much the instructors teach.

<u>Performance</u>

Training was one of the essential functions of a personnel department. The original goal of employee training programs was to improve their performance. Historically, operations and sales are the two departments that require the most training support. Many programs were designed just for sales representatives or operators. The main objective was to enhance the productivity of employees to sell, produce or serve.

The training programs for machine operators are straightforward and often provided by machine suppliers. The procedures of operating machinery can be unique in that different models of the same machine brand need specific training to get the technical know-how of the devices. If the organization has a fleet of machines from the same brand, it may employ and train in-house instructors to do the job. However, hiring trainers from manufacturers is more common for small and medium enterprises.

In service industries, such as hospitality and travel, many corporations have standard operating procedures (SOP) to ensure their services can maintain a high level. All employees must be familiar with the SOP to deliver prompt service with quality. In-house training programs are tailor-made for that purpose, as outsiders would not know their SOP well enough.

Every corporation, including nonprofits, wants to strengthen its sales force. In the past, sales training was focused on salesmanship, such as cold calling, handling objections and closing. Most of the contents were hard-selling skills, which were ineffective as consumers and corporate clients became more and more informed. Some professional sales trainers started to help, offering selling skills workshops that are generic or industry-specific. Many of them focus on soft skills, such as negotiation, active listening, and self-motivation.

Training courses to improve employees' performance can be specialized in certain areas that are commonly found in most organizations, including accounting, human resources, information technology, sales and marketing. Those programs can be in-house or provided by third parties, such as professional associations, educational institutions and consulting firms. Courses offered by those organizations are usually well-recognized within the industry or accredited with a designation or certification.

Today's training covers much more content with many different topics, especially soft skills. Time management, communication skills and positive thinking are some topics that fit every employee. Some training courses, such as leadership, problem-solving and conflict management, are designed to help managers increase their job efficiency and effectiveness. Some of those are also suitable for top management, including critical thinking, equity, diversity and inclusion.

As the learning objectives diversify, many team-building events are introduced to improve the team's spirit, communication, planning, collaboration and leadership skills. Typical events include painting, cooking, and wine and beer-making classes.

Many organizations also organize other learning activities to motivate their employees, build bridges across departments or simply show employees appreciation. Common activities include coffee tasting, guided meditation, yoga or other exercise classes.

Compliance

When the commercial world evolved, many professional bodies were set up to promote the professionalism of their industries. Some codes of ethics were set up for their members to follow. The governments also intervened. Laws were passed at different levels to regulate certain industries, such as banks, charities and transportation. Besides complying with statutes, those industries also have to follow the rules and regulations set up by the corresponding associations or regulatory bodies. The organizations and their employees must comply with all the laws, rules and regulations. At the same time, some organizations have policies for employees to follow to do a better job. Therefore, an organization may have internal and external compliance to deal with, and the organization must provide learning programs for employees to understand all those compliance issues.

Internal compliance learning focuses on the organization's policies that apply to the employees' job responsibilities that the organization wants to ensure the employees fulfill. Internal compliance learning courses are usually taught by in-house trainers of the learning and development section of the human resources department. That is because an external trainer will not know the organization's policies well enough to teach those courses.

External compliance learning focuses on laws, rules, and regulations that apply to the industry that the organization is obligated to comply with. External compliance learning is vital to the organization, as noncompliance may lead to heavy penalties, including massive fines or the organization's license being revoked. In-house trainers or external professionals can teach external compliance learning courses. The trainer must be qualified, and the trainees are typically required to pass an exam to complete the training.

The contents for compliance learning are limited to the basic knowledge required for the employees to do their jobs. For example, accountants of real estate brokerage firms must know the legal requirements for reconciling the trust account. However, they do not have to understand the legal requirements for depositing funds into and withdrawing funds from the trust account, which are the brokers' duties.

Compliance learning will also discuss the rules and regulations employees cannot violate. They must know what they cannot do to comply with the laws. The training is not to enable them to do some jobs but to advise them not to do particular jobs for compliance. For example, in most jurisdictions, frontline staff in a bank cannot sell mutual funds to their clients unless they have a mutual fund license. The banks are responsible for ensuring their employees will not violate such a rule.

Since the purpose of compliance learning is to ensure employees understand all the relevant laws, regulations, and internal policies that govern the organization, the course contents will seldom include extra materials outside the scope of compliance. The advantage is to focus on compliance issues without distracting the learners. The disadvantage is that learners can only get information related to compliance issues and nothing more.

If an organization has compliance issues to deal with, the human resources department should coordinate with other departments that need compliance, such as accounting or sales, to ensure all department staff are well-trained regarding compliance issues. For internal compliance, trainers should be the employees of the organization who have a thorough understanding of the organizational workflow in addition to the subject matters. For external compliance, external expertise can also be sought.

Development

Besides improving the performance of employees or complying with laws, regulations and policies, the purpose of having learning programs for employees also includes building development for the trained employees. That is why the function is called "learning and development". Improvement of the employees' performance and compliance requirements are general development. Development can be for personal, professional, cross-department or verticle too.

Employees need more soft skills for self-development, which are good for the organization and themselves. Employees with improved characteristics can not only do better jobs at work but also improve their lives by having better relationships with family, friends and coworkers.

Professional development is within the employee's profession, such as accounting, information technology, human resources and real estate. For example, junior accounting clerks may want to take courses to get a professional accounting designation, and even experts in the field of information technology may have to take classes to learn about the most advanced technology. Human resources have different specialties, such as compensation and benefits, hiring and recruitment, and learning and development. Like employees in other departments, human resources professionals may want to develop their careers diversely and work in different teams.

Real estate is one of the most diverse fields in the business world. It includes different streams of expertise, from leasing to acquisition and development to facilities management. Many real estate professionals like to be involved in other specialties. A horizontal career move is often seen in the real estate department of many corporations.

Some employees, especially junior employees, may not fit their positions and want to transfer to other departments. Such moves may require fundamental knowledge of that particular field, which the employee may not have. In-house learning programs may serve the purpose of helping those employees change their job positions.

It is common to transfer managers from one department to another, such as from the sales department to the marketing department. However, most organizations may not have learning programs for those managers to learn the necessary knowledge of another department. Even if they have, those managers may not want to learn it through the internal learning programs to let their colleagues and subordinates know that they are not equipped with the necessary knowledge. As a result, external education providers are their choices.

For verticle development, all employees being promoted may need more knowledge or skills for their new jobs after their promotions. There are many learning courses specially designed for managers. Most of them are soft skills, such as team building, decision making and conflict resolution. All those people skills are crucial for managers, especially managers who are new to managing people or a big team.

Top executives need the least learning programs among all managers. However, it is the most challenging task for the human resources department to invite them to take learning and development programs. Unless the CEO thinks some of the executive team members need help to polish their skills, the human resources department will not suggest top executives take any learning and development programs as that is a kind of disrespect or offence. If the CEO needs help, the head of the human resources department is not in a position to take the initiative to make such a suggestion. That responsibility belongs to the board of directors of that organization.

The board of directors will investigate when the organization has a problem with the top management team. If they believe the CEO needs help to polish some skills, they will likely hire an external trainer to do the executive coaching. A consulting firm is typically involved.

4. Different Learning Methods

As the need for training evolves, the methods for trainers to deliver training content change with learners' preferences. Many teaching methods have been developed, from the original passive training mode to more interactive learning manners, and most of them are still being used in training and development. Below are some of the common learning methods used in the field.

Recitation

Recitation is a presentation made by a student to demonstrate knowledge of a subject or to provide instruction to others.[1] It may be the oldest teaching method used in the education field. The typical way of recitation is to let students sit in silence while one student after another takes turns reciting the book or teaching material. The student must read aloud to ensure that everyone in the classroom can listen to it, which also helps the student memorize the contents. This kind of recitation is typically used in primary schools but is seldom used in corporate training.

With advanced technology available, audio or video files of the text are given in class or online at home, so the students can listen to or watch the material at a place that is

---

[1] "Recitation", Wikipedia, last accessed November 8, 2022, https://en.wikipedia.org/wiki/Recitation

convenient to them and at their own pace. Although it may not be very effective and is boring as students are not actively involved in the process, it is still used in some training courses as a one-way teaching method to save resources, such as compliance and technical training.

Lecture

A lecture is an oral presentation intended to present information or teach people about a particular subject.[2] Storytelling may be the initial form of lectures given. The storyteller delivers the story by reading a book aloud or by making a lengthy recitation. While the recitation teaching style mentioned above is typically used in primary schools, the lecture style is used at higher levels, including colleges. The teacher will give a long discussion to cover the whole period, with a one-way conversation on a pre-assigned topic. Students will take notes to memorize critical pieces of information. Occasionally, they will ask questions to clarify some points they do not fully understand.

Lectures are used for activities involving keynote speakers giving a talk to large numbers of employees or students. The advantage of lectures is that they best suit situations with a big audience crowd, as they are one of the most cost- and time-effective teaching methods. However, it is a passive learning mode which does not involve significant

---

[2] "Lecture", Wikipedia, last accessed November 8, 2022, https://en.wikipedia.org/wiki/Lecture

audience participation, as interactions between a large crowd of audience and the lecturer are inconvenient.

Chalk Talk

A chalk talk is an illustrated performance in which the speaker draws pictures to emphasize lecture points and create a memorable and entertaining experience for listeners.[3] Chalk talk is more dynamic as the teacher talks while using real-time illustrations rather than static images. Instead of giving oral lectures alone, most teachers will use chalk to write on the blackboard to highlight and summarize the key points or elaborate on the ideas.

Chalk talk is not limited to using chalk and a blackboard. Improved modern equipment includes transparent plastic films with an overhead projector and dry-erase markers with a whiteboard. The teachers write on the transparent films or whiteboard like on the blackboard. Some will use a printer to print the text on the transparencies in advance. The advantage is time-saving, but the disadvantages are that it is less interactive and lacks flexibility.

Interactive

Interactive learning is a pedagogical approach that incorporates social networking and urban computing into

---

[3] "Chalk talk", Wikipedia, last accessed November 8, 2022, https://en.wikipedia.org/wiki/Chalk_talk

course design and delivery.[4] Unlike teachers giving a one-way speech in the lecture style, teachers in the interactive style will not have questions for themselves and then provide the answers to students after asking. They will ask students questions and wait for the answers. The responses from students may not be correct, and some may even say they do not know. That is perfectly fine, as the purpose of having questions for students is to create interactions.

Simple questions are often used to break the ice. For example, teachers may simply ask the students what they see on the board or screen. More profound questions will then be asked to promote self-discovery and develop problem-solving skills, which can help the student develop a broader and deeper understanding of the topic. Other activities may also be used, such as forming a group and using a flip chart to answer the questions instead of telling the answers individually and orally. It can also facilitate peer-to-peer learning.

Case Study

A case study is an in-depth, detailed examination of a particular case (or cases) within a real-world context.[5] In case study learning, the students are required to read a pre-defined case, which may be a data set, scenario or application. The

---

[4] "Interactive Learning", Wikipedia, last accessed November 8, 2022, https://en.wikipedia.org/wiki/Interactive_Learning
[5] "Case study", Wikipedia, last accessed November 8, 2022, https://en.wikipedia.org/wiki/Case_study

case is accompanied by a list of questions asking students to reflect on the information provided and formulate a response. The questions are often open-ended and may be combined as a problem to be solved. Students are asked to develop a solution to the problem with multiple potential solutions.

A case study is an active learning activity which involves every student. They may be required to study the case and answer the questions individually, and they may be asked to form groups to analyze, discuss, and respond. Case studies best suit students who are more inductive than deductive reasoners, as they learn better from examples than logical development.

Distance Learning

Distance learning, also known as distance education, is the education of students who may not always be physically present at a school.[6] This flexible learning method best suits learners who are out of the country, province or town, or the learner and the teacher are separated in either time or distance. Therefore, it has focused on nontraditional students, such as full-time workers, homemakers, and nonresidents or individuals in remote regions who cannot attend classroom lectures.

Traditionally, distance learning courses are correspondence courses wherein students mail with the

---

[6] "Distance education", Wikipedia, last accessed November 8, 2022, https://en.wikipedia.org/wiki/Distance_education

education provider. Learning materials, such as textbooks, are mailed to students with the assignments. Students are required to read the materials and finish the assignments by the scheduled time. An exam can be arranged at a proctored examination centre as the final requirement to pass a distance learning course.

<u>Online Learning</u>

In the cyber age, most distance learning courses are now conducted via the Internet. Instead of mailing learning materials to students, all relevant materials are stored on the server, and students can download them with a password. Online learning is the name given to distance learning that takes place over the Internet. Online learning is often referred to as "e-learning", among other terms, such as the virtual classroom. However, e-learning is not limited to online learning; it refers to the combined use of computer hardware, software, and educational theory and practice to facilitate learning.[7]

There are a few benefits online learning can bring in addition to its distance learning nature. First of all, it saves all the postage costs of traditional distance learning. It provides a fast and reliable communication channel between learners and teachers via email. Most online courses offer students self-paced learning to better manage their time. Since tests

---

[7] "Educational technology", Wikipedia, last accessed November 8, 2022, https://en.wikipedia.org/wiki/Educational_technology

and exams are also online, students can take them whenever they finish their studies.

Online learning can be recorded videos in which the teachers record their lessons, with or without the presence of the audience. Some online courses are live broadcasts of the classes taught by the teachers. It does not matter which types of online learning courses; they allow teachers more flexibility to manage all course-related matters.

Game-based Learning

Game-based learning is a type of gameplay that has defined learning outcomes. Generally, game-based learning is designed to balance subject matter with gameplay and the ability of the player to retain and apply said subject matter to the real world.[8]

Since the first video game came out, many people have been addicted to it. With the development of the Internet, online games dominated the market. Professional leagues are formed in many countries; most players are Millennials and Generation Z. As a result, many learning programs are designed as games to accommodate new trends and provide more fun ways to learn.

Although the younger generations like gaming more than older adults, game-based learning programs are suitable

---

[8] "Educational game", Wikipedia, last accessed November 8, 2022, https://en.wikipedia.org/wiki/Educational_game#Game-based_learning

for all ages. They are designed in a fun way, and knowledge may be conveyed to the players unwittingly. Game-based learning programs have extra benefits, such as helping develop hand-eye coordination, improving map-reading skills and assisting people who experience attention disorders and dyslexia.

Game-based learning does not have to be online or digital. Games can be created as classroom activities to help learners understand the contents, especially some abstract concepts that are difficult to express verbally.

Blended Learning

Blended learning is also called hybrid learning. Some scholars defined it as an approach to education that combines online educational materials and opportunities for interaction online with physical place-based classroom methods.[9] However, since there is a lack of consensus on a hard definition of blended learning, some define it as a combination of different teaching methods or media. It can be a mixture of classroom teaching and computer-mediated activities to deliver content or a mix of online and in-person content delivery. The computer-mediated or online portion can replace some classroom activities or supplement them.

Blended learning is used in many professional learning and development programs. Since blended learning is a

---

[9] "Blended learning", Wikipedia, last accessed November 8, 2022, https://en.wikipedia.org/wiki/Blended_learning

mixture of two different teaching methods, it may fit more learners than other learning methods. The classroom activities often involve simulations. Scenarios are presented to the learners in the simulation section, who are expected to solve the problems in the class.

Multimedia Learning

Multimedia learning refers to teaching environments that use a combination of different content forms, such as illustrated text, narrated slideshow presentations, charts and graphs, audio, animations, photos, or video, into interactive presentations. Sometimes, games are also included in the lessons.

Studies show that there are a few benefits of using multimedia learning.[10] Learners can absorb more sensory information and commit more of the lesson to memory than traditional learning methods. Since learners are highly stimulated when absorbing images, video, and animations, multimedia can increase student attentiveness and information retention. Multimedia learning tends to be more fun for learners than listening to lectures or reading textbooks; it can increase learners' knowledge and passion for the subject being taught. Furthermore, students and teachers can gather information from diverse sources, allowing them to explore and develop their knowledge mutually.

---

[10] "The Benefits of Multimedia Education", TechRow, last updated March 24, 2022, https://www.techrow.org/blog/the-benefits-of-multimedia-education/

New Trends

Adult education and corporate training are more flexible than children and college education in terms of learning methods. New learning methods are created as supplements or to replace the abovementioned methods. Virtual reality, artificial intelligence and microlearning are some of them.

Actually, virtual reality learning has been used for workplace training for decades to help people build hard skills in some industries. For example, flight simulators with big screens have been used to train pilots for years. Newer versions with headsets are used to train surgeons for complicated surgeries. A study found that virtual reality learners were four times faster to train than those in a physical classroom.[11]

With artificial intelligence used in learning and development, programs can be tailor-fit to match the different learning styles of employees. The big data collected and computed by artificial intelligence can identify the gaps in a learner's knowledge. According to the analysis, the system can create learner profiles to enhance the overall learning experience and teach new skills to that employee.

Microlearning is one of the newest and most welcome methods used in learning and development. Short videos,

---

[11] "What does virtual reality and the metaverse mean for training?", PcW, last updated September 15, 2022, https://www.pwc.com/us/en/tech-effect/emerging-tech/virtual-reality-study.html

articles, podcasts, or practical activities are used to train employees. The main advantage is that the content can be easily absorbed quickly, such as during lunch hour or on a commute. Another advantage is that it fits remote employees, as most microlearning courses are virtual.

5. Course Contents

The contents of learning courses depend on the learning objectives. While the contents are not the same, they are typically classified into two big groups – hard and soft skills. Hard skills are job-related competencies that require specific technical knowledge and training. Soft skills are character traits that affect the way employees work, which can be developed or inborn.

Since hard skills are technical in nature, they are easier to assess than soft skills. Organizations may require professional qualifications for their instructors to teach some hard skills. Some organizations may have to provide more hard skills courses to their employees, while most emphasize soft skills. In general, hard skills

Hard Skills

There are different types of hard skills, and an organization may not require its employees to know all of them or know them in-depth. Specific hard skills required by most organizations include the following topics, sorted by department.

Accounting and Finance

The accounting and finance department is one of the essential departments that an organization has. Employees in the department will be responsible for different functions, such as accounts payable and receivable, payroll and time off, inventory cost management, bookkeeping, budgeting, legal compliance, financial statements and reporting.

Most accounting and finance department employees are certified professionals with qualifications and designations from relevant organizations. Most of them have been trained by third-party education providers or previous employers before joining the organization. However, they may still need courses to update their knowledge or to catch up with the latest practice in the field. For example, an organization may want to change their accounting reporting from GAAP to IFRS, and its accounting personnel may have to learn about the IFRS reporting requirements if they do not have previous experience dealing with that.

Even though the accounting personnel are experienced and competent to do their job, new employees may have to learn the accounting software the organization uses. The organization may use particular software, either third-party packages or tailor-made, that the new employees are not familiar with. They must learn how to use the software before they can prepare financial statements and other reports.

Human Resources

Although human resources is not a legal department, its jobs may have to deal with legal issues, such as employer-employee relations, compensation and benefits, and health and safety. Its team members must have knowledge of employment law, human rights, immigration law, income tax law, occupational health and safety law, and relevant environmental regulations.

Trainers for these topics may be legal professionals such as lawyers and paralegals or experienced human resources professionals who are the subject matter experts, so they are knowledgeable enough to be trainers. For topics that involve special rules and regulations, such as handling and storing inflammable materials, or technical practices involving health and safety, such as providing first aid to injured employees, employees from the relevant departments can be specialist trainers.

Besides the abovementioned legal knowledge, human resources professionals will need other hard skills, such as payroll, hiring and recruitment. Computer literacy is required for most clerical jobs in the human resources department, especially using spreadsheets and databases. Human resources professionals dealing with compensation and employee benefits also need excellent financial skills.

Information Technology

Small and medium organizations may not have an information technology department to take care of their computer needs, but it does not mean they do not have such needs. Large organizations will build their custom software, while small and medium organizations use off-the-shelf software. In all cases, end-users, especially custom software users, must be trained before they can use the software to do their jobs.

Custom software users must be trained by internal staff, but off-the-shelf software is so standard that most employees would have learned it before joining the organization. Still, professional instructors are required to train users in advanced levels of off-the-shelf software, such as Microsoft Office.

Large organizations may have to train their employees to use computer hardware and programming language, especially after an upgrade of hardware or a change of interface. For example, updating the mainframe or server may require the employees to know how to operate and maintain the new equipment. Changing the interface or adding new functions to the system may also require the information technology professionals in the organization to learn new programming languages, such as those for artificial intelligence.

Sales and Marketing

The sales and marketing department is one of the most critical departments in an organization, including nonprofit ones. All organizations must promote the organization's image, provide customer services (if there is no separate department for that purpose) and support the overall business development. Some of the tasks in the sales and marketing department involve traditional hard skills, such as prospecting, market research and pitching.

The very first training that salespersons will receive and must receive is product knowledge. They cannot sell the products or services without knowing their functions, advantages and benefits. It helps them not only to pitch but also to handle objections. All other selling techniques are based on such knowledge.

Traditional marketing skills, such as presentation skills, are still crucial in advertising and marketing. If third-party professionals are not hired to do the jobs, the in-house production team will have to have excellent writing, photo and video editing skills to produce advertising and marketing materials for online content and hard copies.

With the increasing number of online sales and events, social media has become an effective and efficient way to increase exposure, participation and sales. Search engine optimization (SEO) has also become crucial in improving the quality and quantity of website traffic to a website or a web page from search engines, which may involve a cross-department effort to achieve the best result.

From analyzing sales data to customer behaviour, the research team needs excellent analytical skills to study the data accurately and derive conclusions from helping the organization improve its sales and marketing performance. In this big data era, data mining is a hard skill most organizations need for their research teams if third-party experts are not hired.

Soft Skills

Soft skills are required by employees of all professions to perform their jobs better, regardless of their positions. There are different soft skills, and the following are the most common and important types that every employee can benefit from.

Communication

Effective communication can improve the productivity of an organization by saving time and decreasing the possibility of misunderstanding, hence reducing mistakes. It is crucial to convey a message clearly and precisely. Therefore, excellent communication skills are necessary for everyone, especially the management team.

Broadly speaking, communication is the transmission of information. It includes everything that can convey a message – voice, image, text and video. It can be one way, like using a picture or text to convey a message. It can be two ways; the most common example is a dialogue between two persons. Effective communication is more than exchanging or conveying information concisely. It should also share the emotions and intentions behind the information.

Excellent communication skills can deepen interpersonal relations, avoid conflicts, and help improve decision-making. Common communication courses include language skills, technical writing, email writing and effective communication. In-house trainers of the human resources department should be able to handle all of them.

<u>Creativity</u>

Most of the problems in the business world are not mathematics equations that have set rules to find out the answers. Many problems require creative thinking to solve, especially those related to people. That is why most recruiters emphasize that candidates must have creative problem-solving skills.

People always say, "Think outside of the box!" and tell many success stories of using creative thinking methods, but they may not be able to show precisely how to think outside the box. Many scholars in neuroscience and psychology have talked about how our brain works or how it affects our behaviour. However, those studies have nothing to do with creativity training. The relationship is like the one between medical doctors and athletic training. One will not consult a doctor about how to play basketball or football well, although sports are related to our bodies. Similarly, one will not consult a neurologist or a psychologist about creative thinking, although it is related to our brains.

Many people believe that creativity is an innate trait. All thanks to the creative works of the artists, especially the abstract ones. In fact, creative thinking or problem-solving can be trained, and over 99% of new inventions and ideas are based on existing facts or concepts.[12] A good trainer can tell learners how to think systematically, logically and eventually creatively. All in-house instructors of a human resources department will be capable of doing that after proper creative thinking training.

Interpersonal Skills

Interpersonal skills are essential for creating and maintaining meaningful personal relationships, which is crucial for both internal and external relationships. Interpersonal skills are often referred to as social skills, a set of competencies facilitating interaction and communication with others where social rules and relations are created, communicated and changed in verbal and nonverbal ways.[13] People with good interpersonal skills can build healthy relationships with their colleagues to work better as a team and develop robust relationships with clients for better performance.

Employees who lack interpersonal skills will make people around them feel uncomfortable, confused or apathetic. It will cause arguments, disagreements, lack of collaboration, unnecessary conflicts, and poor communication among employees. Eventually, it will cause damage to the organization.

---

[12] Bryan Law, *Differential Cogitation* (Toronto: Fox College of Business, 2020), 5
[13] "Social skills", Wikipedia, last accessed November 8, 2022, https://en.wikipedia.org/wiki/Social_skills

Similar to communication skills, interpersonal skills are required to communicate well with others. Some topics in interpersonal skills courses overlap with those in communication courses, such as the use of language and effective listening. Some topics are designed for particular situations or people, such as conflict resolution, which is crucial for managers. In some extreme cases, an organization may offer or refer their employees to take an anger management course to improve their interpersonal skills.

Leadership

Every organization, department and team needs leaders to lead, direct or influence others. Leadership is essential for managers to inspire, motivate, and set examples for other employees to accomplish organizational tasks and missions.

Leadership involves different soft skills, overlapping with others, including good communication skills, critical thinking, managing conflicts, making decisions, managing people and strategic planning. In particular, executives need charismatic leadership, which can be trained by improving presentation skills, persuasiveness, and charm to lead and influence others.

Leadership is one of the soft skills that can be learned from classroom activities. Through playing different kinds of games, employees can learn not only leadership but also team building, communication and collaboration skills. It is not difficult for the human resources department to organize group activities for competitions, which are excellent opportunities for employees to build friendships and improve their leadership.

Negotiation

Negotiations occur in many places and occasions. They happen at home with parents, at school with teachers, and at the workplace with colleagues and clients. For most employees, the first negotiation at the workplace is to negotiate their job offer.

Employees need negotiation skills not only for dealing with clients but also for solving workplace conflicts. That particular negotiation skill is called conflict negotiation, and it is crucial to an organization. Employees with conflict negotiation skills can resolve a dispute permanently by providing for each side's needs and adequately addressing their interests.

When employees have to collaborate with various counterparts, excellent negotiation skills can help them get the most from the collaboration. People in lobbying also require good negotiation skills to perform their jobs well. Without excellent negotiation skills, it is difficult for them to voice out issues and persuade regulators to recommend changes in industry regulations, procedures and practices. There are many techniques and styles to be used in negotiations. However, some organizations have preferences for particular styles to match their culture. The human resources department should be sensitive to that, especially when external trainers are hired to facilitate learning.

Problem-solving

One may need different hard skills, such as analytical and research skills, to solve a technical problem in engineering, medicine, computer science, and other subjects. However, the soft skills to solve problems in those fields are quite the same, especially in the business world. To be a good problem-solver, one needs creativity, patience, team-building and active listening skills.

Since problem-solving first starts with identifying the issue, that is why it is crucial to have active listening skills and patience to understand the situation and the ultimate goal. For example, managers may have to resolve workplace conflicts. The conflicts may be due to many reasons, such as unclear job roles, unfair treatment or poor work environment. They may be related to people, machines, systems or policies. The managers must patiently listen to the employees involved in the conflicts and communicate well enough to understand the situation to find out the cause and address the issue.

Learning courses for problem-solving skills are a set of soft skills, often including some hard skills such as data gathering, analysis and fact-finding. Most organizations with in-house trainers can provide such courses to their employees, while some will take advantage of external training courses.

Teamwork

Good teamwork skills are not the same as good leadership. One can be a good team member but not necessarily a good team leader. Valuable team members have good communication, time management, listening and collaboration skills. Being collaborative is the most crucial characteristic of a good team member.

Like leadership skills, teamwork skills can be learned through group activities organized by the human resources department. Other soft skills courses can also improve employees' teamwork skills.

Time Management

Everyone has only 24 hours a day, regardless of the seniority of the position in the organization. Hence, efficient use of time becomes an essential skill in work and life, especially for executives who have to manage many people and make critical decisions.

Time management is not about how to do things faster to save time. It involves different soft skills, such as prioritizing work, creating a schedule for activities, setting deadlines, delegating tasks, and rejecting assignments when there are too many.

Blended Skills

Many learning courses, especially non-technical ones, provide employees with opportunities for blended skills learning. For example, problem-solving and time management may involve the use of spreadsheets. Employees must have a basic understanding of using spreadsheets, both local and shared files. As said at the beginning of this chapter, the contents of learning courses depend on the learning objectives, not the type of skill alone. Therefore, most learning courses consist of hard and soft skills, and often more than one from each class.

6. Trends in Learning and Development

The functions and structure of human resources departments have changed a lot since the concept of personnel departments was created. At the same time, the involvement of the learning and development team also has changed with the evolution of the business world and the advancement of technology.

Orientation

It is crucial to introduce new employees to their job roles and work environments. That is the purpose of a corporate orientation. For small and medium enterprises, the new employee's supervisor may do the orientation. For big corporations, the human resources department may have to take over the job as there are other things to let the new employees know, such as the employee benefits, policies, procedures and corporate culture.

Orientation helps new employees get familiarized with the organization and coworkers, too. It may need to assist new employees with installing and operating their technology, such as showing them how to use a custom computer program. Therefore, the orientation may be split into two parts: the human resources department will handle the part related to the whole corporation, and the department supervisor will be responsible for other topics related to the department.

Internal Hiring

It is not uncommon for employees to move from one department to another for jobs that are new to them. There are many reasons for employees to change their positions. Some look for a change of job nature, some look for a new work environment, some look for a higher salary, and some look for a better career path. Many of those employees are willing to stay in the same organization if they can find a suitable position within it. It is a win-win situation for employees to transfer within their organization. The organization can keep the talent, and the employees can lower the risks of taking a new position in an organization that is strange to them.

Most organizations prefer internal hiring as it has other benefits, such as boosting organization loyalty and engagement and saving hiring costs and time. The learning and development team has to work closely with each team leader in the organization to know the opportunity for internal hiring and to provide appropriate learning programs to the employees hired internally.

Reskilling and Upskilling

The learning programs offered to internally hired employees are mainly reskilling and upskilling courses. Those courses can also prepare employees looking for internal transfer or promotion opportunities. Some internally hired employees may be transferred or promoted to a new role where they need extra knowledge or skill sets to be competent in their new positions. Therefore, reskilling or upskilling courses are required to be created for those employees.

Reskilling and upskilling courses are not limited to providing to internally hired employees. Due to a shift in labour from humans to machines, more operators, technicians, and engineers are needed on the production lines instead of human assemblers. Reskilling and upskilling courses are required to transform existing employees from low-skilled to highly-skilled workers, especially for employers in the manufacturing industries.

Equity, Diversity and Inclusion

Equity is the fair and respectful treatment of all people, especially those working for the organization. Diversity mainly deals with demographic issues, focusing on the equal representation of disadvantaged groups, such as minorities, females and the LGBT group. Inclusion concerns people's right to participate and the organization's duty to accept them.

An equitable, diverse, and inclusive environment can promote an organization's image and reputation and enable its employees, contractors, and business partners to reach their full potential and contribute their best by feeling respected, treated fairly, and working in comfortable environments. Therefore, more and more corporations, organizations, and governments are promoting equity, diversity, and inclusion as their core values.

Most organizations establish their culture based on different beliefs, but inclusion is the one that all organizations must set up, promote and maintain. Accepting employees from diverse backgrounds includes providing them with a stressless and comfortable environment without fearing discrimination. If employees feel no equity in the organization, their turnover rate will increase. As a result, more learning courses are required with an increased focus on equity, diversity, and inclusion, especially for management levels. The learning and development team should ensure their organization has such a culture by educating all employees about equity, diversity and inclusion.

Work Ethics

It is crucial for the professionals, such as accountants and lawyers, to act with honesty and integrity. They have to follow a set of rules to protect the public. That is why each professional body has its own code of ethics. Similarly, an organization needs its employees to have good work ethics to protect its best interests.

Work ethics, including trustworthiness, accountability, hard work, dedication, and loyalty, are crucial for every organization. Employees with good work ethics will do their jobs seriously and behave responsibly in a professional setting. All organizations should ensure their employees understand the importance of work ethics through adequate learning programs.

Wellness and Well-Being

All human resources departments must address workplace health and safety issues and comply with occupational health and safety legislation. Those are the basic requirements for maintaining employee well-being. The concept of holistic well-being includes physical, emotional, financial, career and social well-being.

Physical wellness recognizes the need for a safe and healthy work environment for employees to prevent illness and injury. Emotional wellness affects employees' mental health, and stress is the biggest challenge at the workplace. Financial stress affects many employees as they lack money for emergent needs. Career well-being is related to employees' job security and career goals. Social well-being refers to having meaningful friendships in one's personal and work life.

Lacking any of the above wellnesses can prevent employees from enjoying long-term happiness. Besides providing employees with a safe workplace, many organizations also emphasize work-life balance. Some of them offer learning courses to help employees manage their emotions, personal finance, career planning and interpersonal relationships. The bottom line is ensuring employees enjoy working in the organization and live a good life. That is why many large organizations have created the position of Chief Happiness Officer.

Mobile Learning

Mobile learning, also called M-learning, is one of the new trends in learning and development. It is defined as learning across multiple contexts through social and content interactions using personal electronic devices.[14] Although smartphones are widely used for online shopping, ordering food, playing games and learning, the smartphone is not the only personal electronic device used for learning. Notebook computers, smartwatches, and smart TVs can also be tools for mobile learning in any place. Regardless of the tool learners use, the most critical element of mobile learning is focusing on the mobility of learners. Mobile learning allows learners to choose when and where to access learning according to their schedule.

Microlearning is best for mobile learning, but mobile learning is not limited to microlearning. Mobile learning has several benefits. It allows learners to study at their own pace. The learning and development team can develop their content in electronic formats and store them on websites for download or browsing. They can also push the content out to learners on their mobile devices so they can learn whenever they want to study. The learning and development must have resources

---

[14] "M-learning", Wikipedia, last accessed November 8, 2022, https://en.wikipedia.org/wiki/M-learning

to provide mobile learning for their in-house courses, or they can hire external assistance to develop the content in electronic formats.

<u>AI-Assisted Learning</u>

One of the major benefits of mobile learning is that a learner can study at their own pace. The reality is that some learners already have some of the content knowledge, and some are fast learners. Some are visual learners, some are auditory learners, and some are reading and writing learners. They need to study not only at their own pace but also at different content delivery models, speeds, and lengths.

With Artificial Intelligence (AI) technology, a learning program can be modified into different versions to tailor-fit the personal situation of each learner according to their learning habits and results. Artificial intelligence can identify more patterns about learners than the abovementioned distinctiveness. It can use data collected to provide suggestions to content developers to improve how learners learn in real-time.

Some professionals and scholars believe that learning and development in the workplace should be driven by individuals to develop the employees' strengths and skills effectively and that learning and development teams are not supposed to be responsible for employees' development but for listening to each employee's needs and providing the right choices and tools. In fact, learning driven by individuals is the result of AI-assisted learning. With an AI learning system, contents and interfaces will be automatically modified to feed each learner according to their background to optimize the learning experience.

<u>Investing in New Technology</u>

The technology used in learning and development has advanced over the past few decades. From blackboards to whiteboards and transparencies, microfilms and slide projectors to PowerPoint presentations, audio cassette players to compact discs, videotapes to digital video discs, television sets and desktop computers to notebooks and cell phones. Technology will keep improving everyday life as well as business practices. The learning and development teams must catch up with new technology to enhance the learning experience of employees.

With the development of virtual reality, many learning projects can be completed without using physical materials. For example, medical students can perform dissections without using any cadavers. Employees in the construction industry have the opportunity to gain hands-on experience in an indoor environment, a safe, risk-free environment for all seasons.

The cost of using the latest technology can be very high, especially before its maturity phase. The learning and development team may not have to catch up with the latest technologies. However, there are several benefits to using them. For example, medical students using virtual reality technology to practise surgeries may use similar technology to perform operations after graduation using remote surgery hardware and software. However, the development of technology and the installation of related infrastructures, such as 5G highspeed Internet transmission networks, are out of the control of the learning and development team and the organization.

7. From Forced to Voluntary Learning

In the past, continuing education was not mandatory, even in all professional occupations. As society evolved and technology advanced, there was a need for professionals to catch up with the latest developments, laws and technologies in their industries. That made most professional occupations, such as accountants and medical doctors, require their practitioners to undergo continuing education. However, continuing education remains optional in most professions, especially for entry-level positions such as clerks and administrative assistants. Motivating their employees to take learning courses is the main challenge of all learning and development teams.

Employees who have participated or are considering participating in learning programs have different reasons behind their motivation, which can be grouped into the following categories:

Regulatory

Many occupations are regulated in most jurisdictions, such as accountants, engineers and technicians. Organizations with in-house professionals in those regulated businesses must ensure their employees fulfill their mandatory continuing education requirements to maintain their professional qualifications.

Some organizations are big enough to partner with a regulatory body to offer continuing education courses to that regulatory body. They may have hired some professionals from that regulatory body but may not have. For example, a law firm may be able to offer a continuing education course on a newly amended electricity safety law to electrical engineers and electricians. However, the law firm may not have hired any of those professionals.

An employee with a license granted by a regulatory body must fulfill the continuing education requirements of that licensing body. The continuing education courses approved by the licensing authority may be the only learning courses the employee is interested in taking. On the other hand, keeping the license is the only propelling force for that employee to take learning courses.

Continuing education courses of regulatory bodies do not have to be technical knowledge in their field. For example, many mandatory continuing education courses of professional accountant associations are unrelated to accounting. They can be computer courses, management-related, ethics or else.

Since most continuing education programs are credit-based, learners will receive credits for the courses they complete. They have to get a certain number of credits each year or two. Usually, the credits are measured by the hours spent on the learning program and are known as credit hours.

As a result, the learning format can be non-traditional, such as participating in a conference.

The motivation for employees to take mandatory continuing education courses required by regulatory bodies is forced. Most learners take those courses just because they want to maintain their license status. For example, an organization may require its finance manager to have a Certified Public Accountant license. The finance manager is required to maintain the license throughout their employment with that organization. As a result, the finance manager must take appropriate continuing education courses to renew the license.

Since those employees have to take a certain amount of continuing education courses required by their regulatory bodies each year, their interest in taking courses provided by their employers' learning and development teams is reduced. Most of them will not take any learning courses at the workplace unless their employers also make those courses mandatory.

Professional

Unlike regulatory bodies, professional associations do not have the right to grant or revoke professional licenses. They are organizations that provide networking and professional development opportunities to people within specific professions, such as consultants and human resources professionals.

Professional associations provide more networking opportunities for employees who specialize in their industries. Many of them are auxiliaries to the regulatory bodies. Memberships in these associations are voluntary, while memberships in the regulatory bodies are mandatory. For example, bar associations in Canada are nonprofit associations that promote the professionalism of lawyers. The regulatory bodies are the Law Societies in each jurisdiction, which govern Canada's legal profession. The law society, not the bar association, ensures lawyers meet professional standards in its jurisdiction.

Most associations provide continuing education courses to their members. Some of them, like the regulatory bodies, make continuing education mandatory for their memberships. Although joining associations is voluntary, some of the associations are vital to business, and the professionals in that industry must join them.

For example, real estate sales professionals must be licensed in the United States. The Department of State is the regulatory body which issues real estate licenses in that state. The National Association of Realtors is a nonprofit association. It serves licensed real estate salespersons across the United States with subsidiary state associations and local real estate boards. Although a licensed real estate salesperson is not required by law to join the association, over 95% of them joined it.

The main reason is that salespersons, especially those trading residential properties, rely heavily on its Multiple Listings Service (MLS), a private network that allows brokerages to share information on properties they have listed and invite other brokerages to cooperate with them. A salesperson may not be able to trade in real estate without using the MLS system, and joining the association is the only way to use it for doing business.

Since the mission of those trade-related associations is to help their members do business, the continuing education courses provided by associations are typically related to their industry, most of which are hard skills. As a result, association members are more willing to take the courses as it can help them do more business or perform better in their jobs, regardless of whether the courses are mandatory. In other words, the motivation to take association courses is less forced and more voluntary.

Career Development

The learning courses provided by regulatory bodies and professional associations allow employees to get professional licenses or maintain their licenses or memberships. In some sense, the learning courses offer career development opportunities for employees, especially those who need to be licensed to advance their positions. However, the career paths of those employees are decided by licenses offered by the regulatory bodies or the nature of the businesses of the associations.

For example, an employee who wants an accountant license would have planned their career in accounting. Similarly, members of the government employees associations would have intended to develop their careers within the government. However, not all employees want to build their career paths in their current field or within the organization they are currently employed. That is the reason why some employees welcome reskilling and upskilling courses.

Many managers worry that their employees will leave their organizations after they have learned enough knowledge through the courses provided by the organization free of charge. In particular, most of them believe that reskilling and upskilling courses should not be offered to employees because these courses aim to help them find another job elsewhere. However, learning enough knowledge does not cause employees to quit their jobs, and we should not put the cart before the horse.

According to a study, the main reason for Americans to quit their jobs in 2021 was low pay (63%), tied with another cause of no opportunities for advancement (63%), and the third reason was feeling disrespected at work (57%).[15] In other words, no employee will quit if an organization offers

---

[15] "Majority of workers who quit a job in 2021 cite low pay, no opportunities for advancement, feeling disrespected", Pew Research Center, last updated March 9, 2022, https://www.pewresearch.org/fact-tank/2022/03/09/majority-of-workers-who-quit-a-job-in-2021-cite-low-pay-no-opportunities-for-advancement-feeling-disrespected/

decent salaries, has opportunities for advancement, respects them and solves other problems that cause employees to quit. Its employees will not leave the organization no matter how many reskilling and upskilling learning courses they have taken.

There is no doubt that reskilling and upskilling learning courses can attract more employees to enroll. Employees can upgrade their knowledge and be more competitive in the job market, even if they do not have any plans to quit their jobs at the moment. Equipping themselves is a good motivation for the employees to take courses, especially when job security is low. Courses offered by industry-recognized education providers or academic institutions are more attractive to those employees when compared to in-house learning courses.

Industry Recognized

Quality control is one of the keys to success. It gives business partners and customers confidence. That is why many organizations use the ISO 9000 family[16] as their quality management systems standards, as ISO 9000 standards are well recognized in each country. Similarly, employees also want to have well-recognized qualifications to prove their abilities.

Take Microsoft as an example. It offers various certification courses for administrators, analysts, business

---

[16] "ISO 9000", Wikipedia, last accessed November 8, 2022, https://en.wikipedia.org/wiki/ISO_9000

users, engineers, developers and more.[17] It also provides certification courses for trainers. Since its training courses are mainly on Microsoft products, they have the authority to certify learners' knowledge in utilizing its software. Learners can boost their resumes after passing the course exams, so they are more willing to take those courses even if similar courses are available from their employer.

Another tech giant, Google, also offers certification courses in cloud data-related techniques.[18] Some of those online courses do not require learners to have relevant experience to start with them, and some provide professional-level knowledge. That kind of knowledge is crucial to all businesses with an online presence. That is why Amazon[19] and Meta[20] also offer certification courses for online trading and social media topics. Since all organizations, big or small, will have to use the products or services provided by these tech giants, employees with certified qualifications granted from them will be more competitive in the job market. As a result, employees are more willing to take those courses for their own development.

[17] "Microsoft Certifications", Microsoft, last accessed November 8, 2022, https://learn.microsoft.com/en-us/certifications/

[18] "Job-ready skills you can put to work", Google, last accessed November 8, 2022, https://grow.google/certificates/#?modal_active=none

[19] "Training and Certification", Amazon Web Services, Inc., last accessed November 8, 2022, https://aws.amazon.com/training/

[20] "Meta Certification", Meta, last accessed November 8, 2022, https://www.facebook.com/business/learn/certification

Another example is Six Sigma. It is a set of techniques and tools to improve manufacturing quality by identifying and removing the causes of defects and minimizing variability in manufacturing and business processes.[21] It combines Lean Manufacturing[22] and Lean Enterprise[23] to form Lean Six Sigma,[24] aiming to improve organizational performance and eliminate waste processes.

Both Six Sigma and Lean Six Sigma certifications are well-recognized in the business world, but there is no unique accreditor to award the certification. Many education providers offer Six Sigma certification programs through different accreditation authorities. The situation is like Montessori; a teacher can be Montessori certified through different accreditation bodies.

Although organizations may provide some of the industry-recognized courses to their employees if the accreditation authority approves them, most organizations choose not to do it that way. Instead, they will ask their employees to pick external learning courses. It is a better option as it provides flexibility to the employees and reduces

[21] "Six Sigma", Wikipedia, last accessed November 8, 2022, https://en.wikipedia.org/wiki/Six_Sigma
[22] "Lean manufacturing", Wikipedia, last accessed November 8, 2022, https://en.wikipedia.org/wiki/Lean_manufacturing
[23] "Lean enterprise", Wikipedia, last accessed November 8, 2022, https://en.wikipedia.org/wiki/Lean_enterprise
[24] "Lean Six Sigma", Wikipedia, last accessed November 8, 2022, https://en.wikipedia.org/wiki/Lean_Six_Sigma

the resources involved by the learning and development teams.

Academic Recognized

An academic qualification may be the best credential a person can rely on to look for a job, especially a white-collar one. Suppose an organization can offer employees a free part-time study program to earn a Harvard MBA (Master of Business Administration) degree. In that case, the chance is that most employees will be interested.

Many jobs require candidates to have post-secondary education. It may be a degree from a university, a post-graduate certificate from a community college, or a specialty certificate from a private college. Universities are usually publicly funded and offer many degrees in various subjects. Community colleges are also public-funded. Most of their programs are certificate or diploma programs in applied arts and technology, although they may also offer degree programs. Most private colleges are business schools or vocational institutions specializing in specific fields.

All of these higher education institutions provide employees with quality learning opportunities. Many organizations fully subsidize employees if they take courses from colleges that are relevant to their jobs, especially short-term courses. Some will even provide full-cost subsidies with living allowance to employees who choose to advance their studies in selected universities, including full-time MBA programs.

A certificate from a higher education institution is more than an endorsement of the academic achievement of an employee, as getting a certification is a stamp recognizing their expertise and knowledge. That is an excellent motivation to take learning courses, especially when the organization sponsors the learning and for those who have not taken a formal educational program. That makes forced learning turn into voluntary as the learners want to advance their academic achievement.

Many organizations cooperate with colleges to offer their employees tailor-fit programs that are unique in the field. Regardless of the labour market condition, most employers continually scramble to keep top talent. By offering opportunities for certification, an organization is sending a message that it values its employees with long-term career goals. In return, the employees who take the courses will view the organization as a progressive and long-term career employer.

Incentives

To make employees willing to learn, many organizations offer incentives for them to take learning courses, especially in-house ones. Some of them think free learning is a good incentive, but they are wrong. We have never seen one in-house learning course that would cost employees a fee. However, not many employees are interested in taking in-house learning courses unless they are mandatory.

Some organizations offer credit money for employees to choose the learning courses they like. It is not a cash benefit but a credit to be used for learning courses only. That is, employees cannot use the money elsewhere but can use the money to pay for the learning courses they like. Some organizations allow the credit to be applied to personal interest classes, such as swimming and Pilates, for better work-life balance and mental health.

Some organizations offer a raise in salary for employees, including a raise in the hourly rate charged by independent contractors who finished specific courses that can improve their work performance. For example, employees and independent contractors in the information technology department may have a raise in their salary or hourly rate if they complete specific industry-recognized certification IT courses.

A Japanese company started offering six extra days off per year to non-smoking employees in 2017.[25] It introduced the policy after an employee complained about cigarette breaks affecting productivity, as the breaks would usually last

---

[25] "This Japanese company is giving employees who don't smoke 6 extra vacation days", CNBC, last update November 2, 2017, https://www.cnbc.com/2017/11/02/this-japanese-company-is-giving-non-smokers-6-extra-vacation-days.html

15 minutes, which led to resentment amongst employees who don't smoke. As a result, the CEO decided to give non-smokers some extra time off to compensate. The additional advantage the policy brought was to encourage employees to quit smoking through the incentive of having six extra days off. A company in the United Kingdom liked the idea and rewarded non-smoking employees with four additional vacation days a year to encourage them to quit smoking.[26] Both companies have promising results.[27][28]

Similar policies can be used to encourage employees to take learning courses. Smoking is addictive and difficult to quit. If such a policy can succeed in encouraging employees to quit smoking, it should work in encouraging employees to learn, too.

[26] "Non-smokers at U.K. company rewarded 4 extra vacation days a year", CTV News, last updated January 13, 2020, https://www.ctvnews.ca/business/non-smokers-at-u-k-company-rewarded-4-extra-vacation-days-a-year-1.4764562?cache=%3FclipId%3D86116

[27] "This Japanese Company Gives Non-Smoking Employees Extra 6 Days Off Every Year", Indiatimes, last updated March 11, 2022, https://www.indiatimes.com/worth/news/japan-company-piala-gives-extra-six-days-off-to-non-smoking-employees-564208.html

[28] "U.K. company gives non-smokers 4 more vacation days to promote healthy workplace", Global News, last updated January 14, 2020, https://globalnews.ca/news/6408568/uk-company-vacation-days-smokers/

8. Career Path Development

The organizational chart of a small organization is simple, while the one for an international organization can be very complicated. How an organizational chart is set up will affect the efficiency of the operation of the organization and talent retention.

The simplest method for dividing human resources may be the one that the Mongol Empire used in the 13th century. The Mongolian army was divided into decimal subsections of Arban (10 soldiers), Zuuns (100), Mingghans (1000), and Tumen (10,000).[29] The head of an Arban managed ten soldiers, the head of Zuun managed ten Arbans, the commander of Mingghan supervised ten Zuuns, and the commander of Tumen supervised ten Mingghans. The marshal would command all Tumen heads, often less than ten.

One of the benefits of such a military organization was that each leader would lead ten or fewer persons at each rank, so it was manageable and efficient. Furthermore, a leader's performance can easily stand out from the ten warriors in the same rank, making it easier to get promoted. However, it is not that simple in the modern business world.

---

[29] "Mongol Empire", Wikipedia, last accessed November 8, 2022, https://en.wikipedia.org/wiki/Mongol_Empire

Take a restaurant as an example; most employees belong to the kitchen and floor departments, while managers and bartenders are the minorities. The ratio is often greater than ten. For a small manufacturer, the workers in the factory are the majority, with all other department staff as minorities. The structure of a small business is typically simple. However, it may be the most efficient setup as the owner is often involved in a two-level organization chart – everyone reports to the owner. We will use typical company sizes as examples to study how the organization charts can be created to give all employees a fair opportunity for promotion.

Local Organization

Assuming that an independent restaurant has only one location in a city. The owner is the CEO, the spouse is the CFO, and their kids are the COO and Chief Chef. The first question is: What positions can the non-family employees be promoted to? As family members fill all the senior positions, the first impression is that other employees will not have many opportunities, at least not in C-level positions. There may be no room for their staff to be promoted to the management team. The main incentive for them to stay may be remunerations.

Any family-owned business has the same problem – non-family members find it difficult to get promoted to senior management. When an executive makes a severe mistake, there will be no disciplinary action against that family member, meaning there will be no dismissal and no vacancy for promoting a non-family member employee. That is a crucial issue that the owner must address.

Even for a non-family-owned business, a small company may not be able to offer many levels for its employees to develop their careers as the big corporations do. However, one can create the positions without costing more resources, such as higher salaries and more benefits. Giving employees titles higher than their actual positions is a way to recognize and honour their contributions to the organization.

Using external titles is common practice in big corporations, especially for the sales forces. Many fresh graduates will hold the title "assistant vice president" or "associate vice president" of their sales department once they join the company. They are, in fact, the junior sales representatives of the company. The primary purpose of giving them a higher title is to provide a better image for them to talk to the executives of their client firms. The CEO or CFO of a client firm will be more willing to speak to an assistant vice president of a supplier than to a sales representative or account manager.

Regional Organization

When an organization can be expanded to a regional level, it means the organization has two or more locations to serve its clients and should have a double-digit number of employees. Its organizational chart should be more flexible, and more levels can be created and added to the existing one.

How to create new positions depends on the nature of the organization. For example, a restaurant or retail business that operates at several locations in the same region may need an area manager to oversee and coordinate the operations of all sites. Similarly, a regional sales manager or director may be required to supervise sales teams in all offices.

Different locations of an organization should have the same organizational chart, but it does not mean that every position must be filled. For example, an organization has three levels of managers – from probationary to senior. One location may have a senior manager, another may have no senior manager, and others may have only probationary managers. The headquarters of the organization may have a general manager, but not the other locations.

The significant difference between the organizational charts of a local organization and a regional organization is that a regional organization can offer positions at the regional level. Titles such as area supervisor, regional director or branch manager can be added to create more positions for the employees to be promoted.

National Organization

A national organization can offer more than one position at the regional level, such as several regional managers and directors. It can divide the country into different regions, which may not be the provinces or municipalities. It can use populations, land sizes or travelling time to define a region. However, when defining the regions, efficient management of regional establishments and customer convenience must be considered.

Different regions may have various populations, sales revenues or needs. As a result, the sizes of different regional establishments may not be the same. Therefore, the number of employees will not be the same, so not all the positions will be filled in every establishment. On the other hand, the organizational chart should be the same for each establishment in every region to give employees more opportunities to grow.

Multinational Organization

A multinational organization has operations in more than one country. Therefore, the organization can add more titles based on its multinational characteristics, such as a country manager. Although the organizational chart should be the same in each country where the organization has operations, not every title can be copied from one country to another. In other words, some positions in one country may be unique and will not be filled in other countries.

Under Chinese law, any organization with three or more party members must provide the necessary conditions for cadres to establish a party cell.[30] A party cell is a small committee or group of Chinese Communist Party members within an organization. Members meet regularly to study the party-approved political theory and may engage in other activities as directed by party offices. Although the party cell employees do not hold extra positions in the organization, the party cell is part of the organization chart and may influence the organization's decisions.

Although that kind of arrangement only happens in China, similar requirements may appear in other countries for political or religious reasons. On the other hand, many organizations have advisory committees to provide non-binding strategic advice to the management in order to guide the organization more effectively. Organizations should encourage their employees to apply for positions on their advisory committees to contribute more to the organization. Moreover, being an advisory committee member is a kind of recognition that will add value to the employee's resume.

Global Business

A multinational organization may have operations on the same continent, while a global business will have operations in several countries and on more than one

---

[30] "Command and control: China's Communist Party extends reach into foreign companies", The Washington Post, last updated January 28, 2018, https://www.washingtonpost.com/world/asia_pacific/command-and-control-chinas-communist-party-extends-reach-into-foreign-companies/2018/01/28/cd49ffa6-fc57-11e7-9b5d-bbf0da31214d_story.html

continent. Therefore, it will have more titles for employees to fit their geographic location, such as VP – North American and Executive Director – APAC.

Depending on the size of the organization, each country may have a complete organizational chart that includes the top management team, which may be the same in every country. It may have a CEO in each country, plus a CEO for a continent, then a CEO for its international operation. These job titles are not simply external; they reflect the actual job responsibilities and the geographic regions to which the executives are accountable.

Similar to external titles, internal grades can be used for promoting employees without changing their job descriptions. For example, an organization may have five levels for financial analysts. On their business card, all their titles are the same – Financial Analyst. However, they will be internally ranked into five levels, from Financial Analyst I to Financial Analyst V.

Internal pay grades can also be used for promoting employees without changing their job titles. Many big corporations and governments have internal pay grades to tell the level of seniority of their employees in the organization. For example, the pay grades for junior clerks may be from 1 to 4, senior clerks from 5 to 8, analysts from 6 to 10, accounting managers from 11 to 15, and so forth. The pay grades can overlap, such as when senior clerks are overlapped with analysts.

The pay grades can be confidential, and only human resources and the accounting department can access the confidentiality. It can also be disclosed to everyone to bring the benefits below. One of the benefits of revealing pay grades is easy comparisons of compensation plans for different employees so that they know where they are on the career ladder. Since the pay grades of analysts are from 6 to 10, junior analysts will know that there are four more levels to raise their salary if they are not promoted and stay in the same position, which creates room for them to "develop".

Another benefit is that it provides a transparent structure to everyone involved; for example, taxpayers can tell how much the government pays its employees. The transparency of pay grades for government jobs can also attract talent to apply for the jobs as the entry grade and salary are fully disclosed to the public. For private organizations, if the pay grades of plant technicians and accounting managers are both 11 to 15, the technicians can tell they are at the same seniority levels as accounting managers as their pay grades are the same. That may let the technicians know they are at the manager grades, although their title is not a manager.

The disadvantage of using pay grade is that employees can tell, more or less, how much money their coworkers are making, especially when they are in the same range of pay grades. The pay grades of government employees may be known to the public in many countries, but private organizations may have concerns about privacy issues. Using the above example, a plant technician may know the approximate salary of an accounting manager since their pay grades are the same.

9. Conclusion

Many employees quit their jobs because of a lack of career development. Organizations must help their employees grow together by providing different kinds of support. Offering or sponsoring learning courses is one of the best ways to help employees do their jobs better and develop their careers.

The main functions of a learning and development department are to provide learning opportunities to employees, enrich their knowledge and skills, improve their personal cultivation, and help them develop their careers within the organization. The aim is to align employee goals and performance with the organization. To the surprise of many people, the ultimate objective of a learning and development department is to retain talents.

While all organizations want to reduce their employee turnover rates, the truth is that not every employee is worth keeping. How to determine the value of employees is beyond the scope of this book. However, the learning and development programs can be used to tell the differences among employees. It is not difficult to tell how much the employees have gained from the learning programs. By providing learning programs, we can also determine the attitudes of employees – how eager they are to learn and develop themselves.

Learning programs provide employees not only opportunities to get knowledge and skills to apply to their jobs but also opportunities for personal and career development. Once employees are well-trained, have learned more knowledge, or have become more skillful, they can take on more responsibilities and be promoted to higher positions. Those are the developments for both employees and their organization.

Many people do not want to take continuing education because they have no incentive to do that or the courses are uninteresting. Organizations should try their best to encourage employees to take learning courses by providing incentives. If the courses are in-house ones, they should make them more enjoyable too.

Knowledge and skills to employees are like minerals to plants, to make them healthy and strong. Learning courses are like fertilizers to feed them the necessary nutrients and help them grow. By offering industry-recognized learning programs to employees, organizations give them opportunities to grow with the organizations and independently so that they are more competitive in the job market. It is one of the ways to turn forced learning into voluntary learning, and it is a more effective learning mode.

As discussed in Chapter 8, organizations should create more positions to promote their employees. Most of those positions can be expanded horizontally so that the hierarchy will be simple. For example, a junior analyst can be promoted to an analyst, then a senior analyst without changing the responsibility, but just a minor increase in salary.

Team leads, supervisors, managers and directors are the titles for roles in helping to manage a group of employees and ensuring they meet organizational goals. There is a limit to how well a leader can manage people. One cannot pay attention to too many people, discuss with them and manage their performance. Therefore, the concept of dividing teams should be like the one the Mongol Empire used to manage its army – for each small group of people, there should be a leader to lead the group. That is how more titles can be used to promote employees.

To conclude, organizations must provide attractive learning programs to their employees to give them opportunities to enrich their knowledge and skills. On the other hand, organizations must also provide opportunities for employees to develop their careers within the organizations, especially when the employees are trained and developed. That is one of the ways to retain talent.

Appendix. Human Resources Glossary

Ableism: discrimination and social prejudice against people with disabilities or who are perceived to have disabilities. Ableism can be conscious or unconscious and is embedded in communities, institutions, systems, or society's broader culture.

Absence: a period in which an employee is not working. Absences can be paid or unpaid, depending on the reason for the absence.

Absence Management: a process used to reduce employee absenteeism through policies and procedures.

Absenteeism: refers to the habitual or frequent absence of an employee from work, excluding paid time off.

Accessibility: a general term for the degree of ease that something (e.g., building, device, service, and information) can be accessed, used and enjoyed by persons with disabilities. Easy accessibility benefits the general population, such as seniors and families with small children, by making things more usable and practical for everyone.

Accessible: does not have obstacles for people with disabilities — something that can be easily reached or obtained; facilities that can be easily entered; information that is easy to retrieve.

Adaptive Technologies: the technologies used in some products to help people with vision, hearing, mobility or other disabilities use the products.

Adverse Impact: having a harmful result. Treating people with and without disabilities the same will have a negative effect on some people.

Affirmative Action: an action designed to address the historical disadvantage that identifiable groups (e.g., women and visible minorities) have experienced by increasing their representation in employment, higher education or treatment.

African American/Canadian: an American/Canadian of African origin or descent.

Ageism: stereotyping against individuals or groups based on their age, generally with discrimination.

Agile: a method that moves away from a rules-based and planning-based approach toward a more straightforward and faster model driven by participant feedback.

Alternate Dispute Resolution (ADR): refers to processes designed to facilitate a resolution between two parties in dispute to avoid litigation.

Alternative (Alternate) Format: a method of communication that considers the disability of a person, such as an audiobook instead of a print version for someone with a visual disability.

Annual Leave: a period of paid time off work granted by employers to employees annually to use for whatever they wish, also known as paid time off.

Anti-racism (Anti-oppression): an active and consistent process of change to eliminate racism and the oppression and injustice racism causes.

Applicant Tracking System (ATS): a system that helps organizations organize and track candidates for hiring and recruitment purposes.

Assistive Device: a device to help people, primarily people with disabilities, perform tasks, such as an assistive listening device, forklift and wheelchair.

Attendance Tracking Software: software that helps employers deal with information regarding the hours their employees have worked.

Audism: a belief that a person is superior or inferior based on their ability to hear or act like someone who hears.

Audit: refers to Human Resources Audit

Barrier: anything that prevents a person from fully taking part in all aspects of society, including physical, information or communications, attitudinal, economic and technological barriers, and policies or practices.

Benchmarking: comparing an organization's performance figures against a standardized set of metrics to judge how the organization is doing.

Benefits and Compensation: the benefits that employees receive for working. They can be monetary, rewards-based, medical benefits, retirement, time in lieu, discounts, wellness programs, and more.

Bereavement Leave: provides employees with paid leave in the event of the death of a relative.

BFOR: an acronym for Bona Fide Occupational Requirement, a defence used in discrimination in employment.

Bias: a predisposition, prejudice or generalization about a group of persons based on characteristics or stereotypes.

Bigotry: obstinate or unreasonable attachment to a belief, opinion, or prejudice against a person or people based on stereotypes related to age, race, religion, sexual orientation, and more.

Biological Sex: the biological classification of people as male or female. Sex terms are "male", "female", and "intersex". A doctor assigns sex at birth by visually assessing external anatomy.

Biracial: a person whose ancestry includes members of two racial groups.

Bisexual: a person who is emotionally, physically, sexually or spiritually attracted to more than one gender member.

Black: a social construct referring to people with dark skin colour or other racialized characteristics. Diverse societies apply different criteria to determine who is Black.

Burnout: Feelings of energy depletion or exhaustion due to prolonged and excessive stress tied to jobs.

Caste System: a form of social stratification with roots in India's ancient history and persisting to the present. This system divides its people into four classes: Brahmin, Kshatriya, Vaishya, and Shudra. In addition to the four major castes, another type of people called Dalit or untouchable is excluded from the castes.

Caucasian: an outdated term that has often been used as a synonym for white.

Characteristics: a personal trait or attribute.

Civil Union: a legally recognized arrangement similar to a marriage, created primarily as a means to provide legal recognition for same-sex couples.

Code: refers to the human rights code of the local jurisdiction.

Coming Out: the often life-long process of discovering, defining and proclaiming one's sexuality (usually non-heterosexual).

Competing Rights: situations where parties to a dispute claim that the enjoyment of an individual or group's human rights and freedoms, as protected by law, would interfere with another's rights and freedoms.

Confidentiality Agreement: spells out how to appropriately handle and treat confidential information during and after employment with an employer, also known as a Non-disclosure Agreement (NDA).

Contract: refers to the employment contract.

Culture: the achievements, behaviours, beliefs or customs of a particular time or people; behaviour within a particular group.

Cultural Competence: an ability to interact effectively with people of different cultural or ethnic backgrounds.

Culturally Competent Organization: an organization that displays cultural competence in its systems and individual behaviour.

Custom: a traditional practice.

Data Privacy: the protection of employees' personal information throughout the data lifecycle.

Dimensions of Diversity: the unique personal characteristics that distinguish people as individuals and groups. These include but are not limited to age, gender, race, sex, ethnicity, physical and intellectual ability, class, creed, religion and sexual orientation.

Disability: a broad range and degree of conditions, some visible and some not visible. A disability may have been present from birth, caused by accident, or developed over time. There are physical, mental, cognitive, and learning disabilities; mental disorders; hearing or vision disabilities; epilepsy; drug and alcohol dependencies; environmental sensitivities; and other conditions.

Discrimination: treating someone unfairly by either imposing a burden on them or denying them a benefit, privilege or opportunity enjoyed by others because of their characteristics such as age, religion, family status, disability, sex and race.

Document Management System: a system (software) used to help acquire, manage and store essential documentation for employees in an organization.

Duty to Accommodate: people identified by human rights law are entitled to the same opportunities and benefits as everybody else.

East Asian People: people who share ancestry, heritage and culture from several countries and regions, including China, Hong Kong, Japan, Macau, Mongolia, North Korea, South Korea, Taiwan and Vietnam.

EDI: the abbreviation of Equity, Diversity and Inclusion.

Employer Branding: the process of managing and influencing an employer's reputation among job seekers, employees and key stakeholders.

Employment Contract: a contract used to define the employment terms and workplace rules, which is used as a reference guide in case of a disagreement.

End of Employment (Document)

The document given to employees when their contract ends proves there are no debts between the company and the worker.

Equal Opportunity: to ensure that all people have equal access, free of barriers, equal participation and equal benefit from whatever an organization offers.

Equal Treatment: treatment that brings about equality of access, such as providing a ramp for wheelchair access to a building in addition to a stair.

Equitable: just or characterized by fairness or equity.

Equity: the quality of fairness, impartiality, and even-handedness.

Ethnicity: sharing a distinctive cultural and historical tradition associated with ancestry, creed, place of origin or race.

Exclusion: denying or limiting access to a place, group, privilege, and more.

Furlough: a temporary leave of absence, and the employee is expected to return to work.

Gay: persons who have an emotional, physical, sexual or spiritual attraction to persons of the same sex.

Gender: the social classification of people as masculine or feminine.

Gender Identity: the conscious sense of maleness or femaleness of a person. This sense of self is separate and distinct from one's biological sex.

Harassment: engaging in the course of comments or actions known (or ought reasonably to be known) to be unwelcome. It can involve words or actions known (or ought reasonably to be known) to be demeaning, embarrassing, humiliating, offensive, or unwelcome.

Hate Activity: negative comments or unfriendly actions against a person or group motivated by bias, prejudice or hate based on, including but not limited to, age, ancestry, race, ethnic origin, language, colour, religion, mental disability, physical disability, family status, marital status, sex, sexual orientation.

Heightism: prejudice or discrimination against individuals based on height.

Heterosexual: persons who have an emotional, physical, sexual or spiritual attraction to persons of the opposite sex.

Heterosexism: a belief that heterosexuality is superior and preferable to other sexualities and that heterosexuality is the only right, normal or moral expression of sexuality.

Historical Disadvantage: a disadvantage that results from historical patterns of institutionalized and other forms of systemic discrimination.

Homosexual: an outdated term for persons with an emotional, physical, sexual or spiritual attraction to persons of the same sex. It is more of a medical term and may insult lesbian and gay people or the LGBT community.

Homophobia: the irrational aversion to, fear or hatred of people who are identified or perceived as lesbian, gay, bisexual or transgender (LGBT).

HR Metrics: the key performance indicators used to evaluate the efficiency and effectiveness of various HR responsibilities and initiatives, such as hiring, employee retention, training, and labour costs.

Human Capital Management (HCM): instead of calculating the cost of maintaining human resources, the concept of HCM is to maximize the value of human capital. It converts traditional HR functions into opportunities that increase efficiency, interest and revenue.

Human Resources Audit: an objective examination of HR policies, practices, and procedures to identify points for improvement and ensure compliance.

Impairment: a physical, sensory, intellectual, learning or medical condition, including mental illness, that limits functioning or requires accommodation.

Inclusion: appreciating and using our unique differences – strengths, talents, weaknesses and frailties – to show respect for the individual and ultimately create a dynamic multi-dimensional community.

Inclusive Design: considering differences among individuals and groups when designing something to avoid creating barriers. Inclusive design can apply to systems, facilities, programs, policies, services, education, and more.

Indigenous Peoples: a collective name for the native people who inhabited a country or a geographical region at the time when people of different cultures or ethnic origins arrived.

Intellectual Disability: also called a developmental disability, involves significant limitations in intellectual functioning (reasoning, learning, problem-solving) and adaptive behaviour, which covers a range of everyday social and practical skills.

Intergenerational: existing or occurring between different generations of people, involving more than one generation.

Intermittent Leave: a series of absences that are spread over a period of time rather than taken back to back.

Intersex: a term used for various conditions in which a person is born with a genital that does not seem to fit the typical definitions of female or male, formerly inappropriately referred to as hermaphrodites. Most intersex people do not possess "both" sets of genitals but rather a blending or a different appearance that is medically difficult to categorize for many doctors.

Job Evaluation: tools used to measure the quality of a job and to determine the worth of the job.

Lesbian: a woman who has an emotional, physical, sexual or spiritual attraction to other women.

LGBT: an acronym for Lesbian, Gay, Bisexual and Transgender. Sometimes, GLBT is also used.

LGBTTIQQ2A: an acronym for Lesbian, Gay, Bisexual, Transgender, Transsexual, Intersex, Queer, Questioning, 2-spirited and Allies.

Merit: picking a candidate for a position who meets job-related selection criteria, such as experience, knowledge and skills, at the level required for a position or assignment.

MSM: an abbreviation of Men who have Sex with Men.

Multiracial: a person whose heritage includes members of multiple racial groups.

Native Groups: Indigenous people in the United States.

Non-disclosure Agreement (NDA): see Confidentiality Agreement.

Newcomers: New immigrants in countries of immigration, such as Australia, Canada and the United States.

Organizational Chart: a chart to show the internal structure of an organization, the hierarchy and the competencies of roles within that organization.

Overtime: refers to additional pay for hours worked beyond the standard work hours per week (40 hours in most jurisdictions)

Pay Equity: the principle of equal pay for work of equal value. For example, the principle is applied to pay male and female employees within the same organization the same salary for work that is judged to be of equal value.

Performance Appraisal: tools used to measure the abilities and skills of an employee.

Permanent Employment: the employment contract does not expire and remains valid until the employer or employee decides to end the employment relationship.

Persons of Colour: an inclusive term encompassing a range of social identity groups based on skin colour, such as Asians, Aboriginal Peoples, Hispanics and Blacks.

Persons with Disabilities: persons with one or more long-term or recurring disabilities.

Poisoned Work Environment: a negative, hostile or unpleasant workplace due to comments or conduct that tends to demean a group identified by one or more prohibited grounds under any human rights law or code, even if not directed at a specific individual.

Power: access to privileges such as connections, decision-making, experience, expertise, resources, knowledge and information, enhancing a person's chances of getting what they need to live a comfortable, safe, productive and profitable life.

Prejudice: affective feeling or negative prejudgment about another person or group of persons based on perceived characteristics.

Pride: a term used about the LGBT community. It means people not being ashamed of themselves or showing their pride to others by "coming out", marching in the Pride parade or similar parades, and being honest and comfortable about who they are.

Pride Parade: an outdoor event that celebrates LGBT achievements, legal rights, pride, self and social acceptance

Privilege: unearned access, advantages, benefits, opportunities or power that exist for members of the dominant groups in society. It can also refer to the relative privilege of one group compared to another.

Prohibited Grounds (Protected Grounds): the personal characteristics that the human rights law is based on to prohibit discrimination or harassment. The common protected grounds include age, ancestry, citizenship, colour, creed, disability, ethnic origin, family status, gender identity and gender expression, marital status, place of origin, race, receipt of public assistance (in housing), a record of offences (in employment), sex and sexual orientation.

Queer: formerly derogatory slang term used to identify sexual and gender minorities who are not heterosexual.

Questioning: exploring one's own sexual or gender identity, looking at such things as upbringing, expectations from others, such as friends and employers, and inner motivation.

Race: a group of people with similar geographic, historical, political, economic, physical, social, and cultural factors.

Racialization: the process by which societies construct races as real, different and unequal in ways that matter and affect economic, political and social life.

Racial Profiling: any action that relies on stereotypes about race, ancestry, colour, ethnicity, religion or place of origin, or a combination of these, rather than on a reasonable suspicion to single out a person for greater scrutiny or different treatment.

Racism: a belief that one race group is superior or inferior to others.

Recruitment Costs: the total costs related to sourcing, hiring, and onboarding new talent.

Remote Workers: Employees who work outside the office, either work from home, at the client's office or while travelling.

Self-assessment: personal evaluation of oneself during the performance appraisal process.

Severance Pay: the compensation and benefits an employer provides an employee after the employment is terminated, usually through no fault of the employee.

Sexism: a belief that one gender type is superior or inferior to another, usually linked with discrimination.

Sexual Orientation: the direction of one's sexual interest or attraction. It covers the range of human sexuality from lesbian and gay to bisexual and heterosexual.

South Asian: a native or inhabitant of the Indian subcontinent, including Afghanistan, Bangladesh, Bhutan, India, the Maldives, Nepal, Pakistan, and Sri Lanka.

Stereotype: incorrect assumption based on age, sex, race, colour, ethnic origin, religion, and more. Stereotyping typically involves attributing the same characteristics to all members of a group regardless of their differences.

Straight: an informal term for Heterosexual.

Systemic Barrier: a barrier embedded in the administrative or social structures of an organization, including the culture of an organization, decision-making processes, the physical accessibility of an organization, and organizational policies and practices. The barrier may exclude members of groups protected by human rights law.

Systemic Discrimination: patterns of behaviour, policies or practices that are part of the social or administrative structures of an organization and which create or perpetuate a position of relative disadvantage for groups identified under the human rights law.

Talent Management: anticipating required human capital for an organization and planning to meet those needs.

Toxic Work Environment: same as Poisoned Work Environment.

Turnover Rate: the percentage of employees who leave the organization within a given period (usually one year).

Transgender (or Trans): a person whose biological sex assigned at birth does not match their gender identity.

Transsexual: persons who are identified at birth as one sex but who identify themselves differently and have undergone

one or more medical treatments to align their bodies with their internally felt identity. While some people embrace this term as an identity, it is rejected by others.

Two-Spirit: a term that refers to Aboriginal people who are gay, lesbian, bisexual, or trans-gendered.

Union (Work Union): a formal organization that represents workers to negotiate with the employer involving working conditions, wages, benefits, and other conditions of employment.

Unlimited PTO: a policy that offers employees an undefined amount of paid time off, requested at the description of the employee and approved by a superior.

Virtual HR: using technology to provide employees with self-service options and assist the human resource department with the automation of everyday tasks.

WFH: abbreviation for Work From Home.

White: people belonging to various peoples with light-coloured skin, usually of European origin. The term has become an indicator less of skin colour and more of racialized characteristics.

Zero-Based Budgeting: a budgeting technique in which all expenses must be justified for a new period and start from zero.

www.ingramcontent.com/pod-product-compliance
Lightning Source LLC
Chambersburg PA
CBHW071605200326
41519CB00021BB/6875